BLACK POWERFUL AND GORGEOUS

An Adult Coloring Book For Black Women

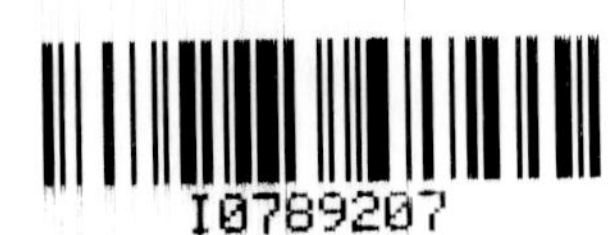

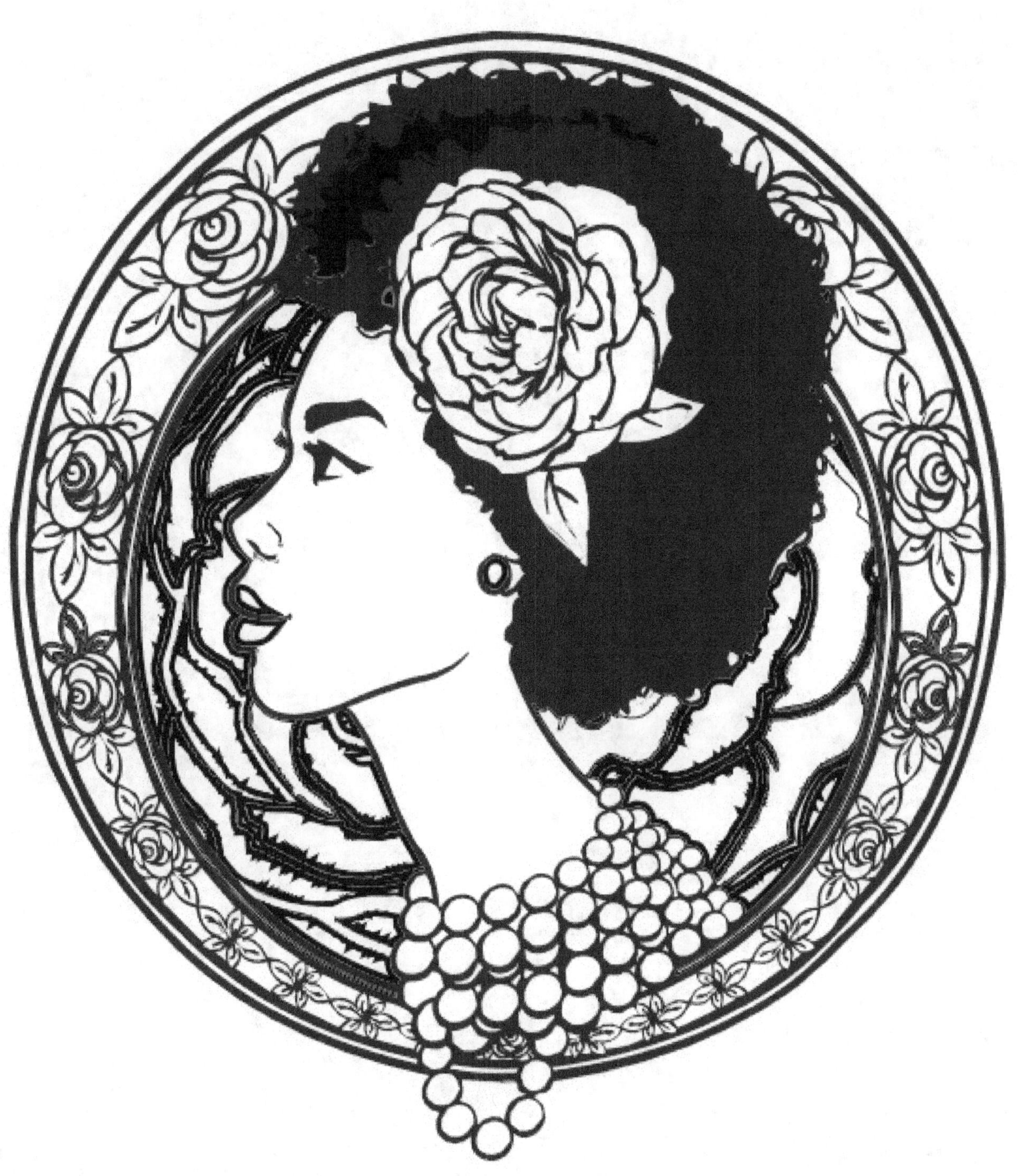

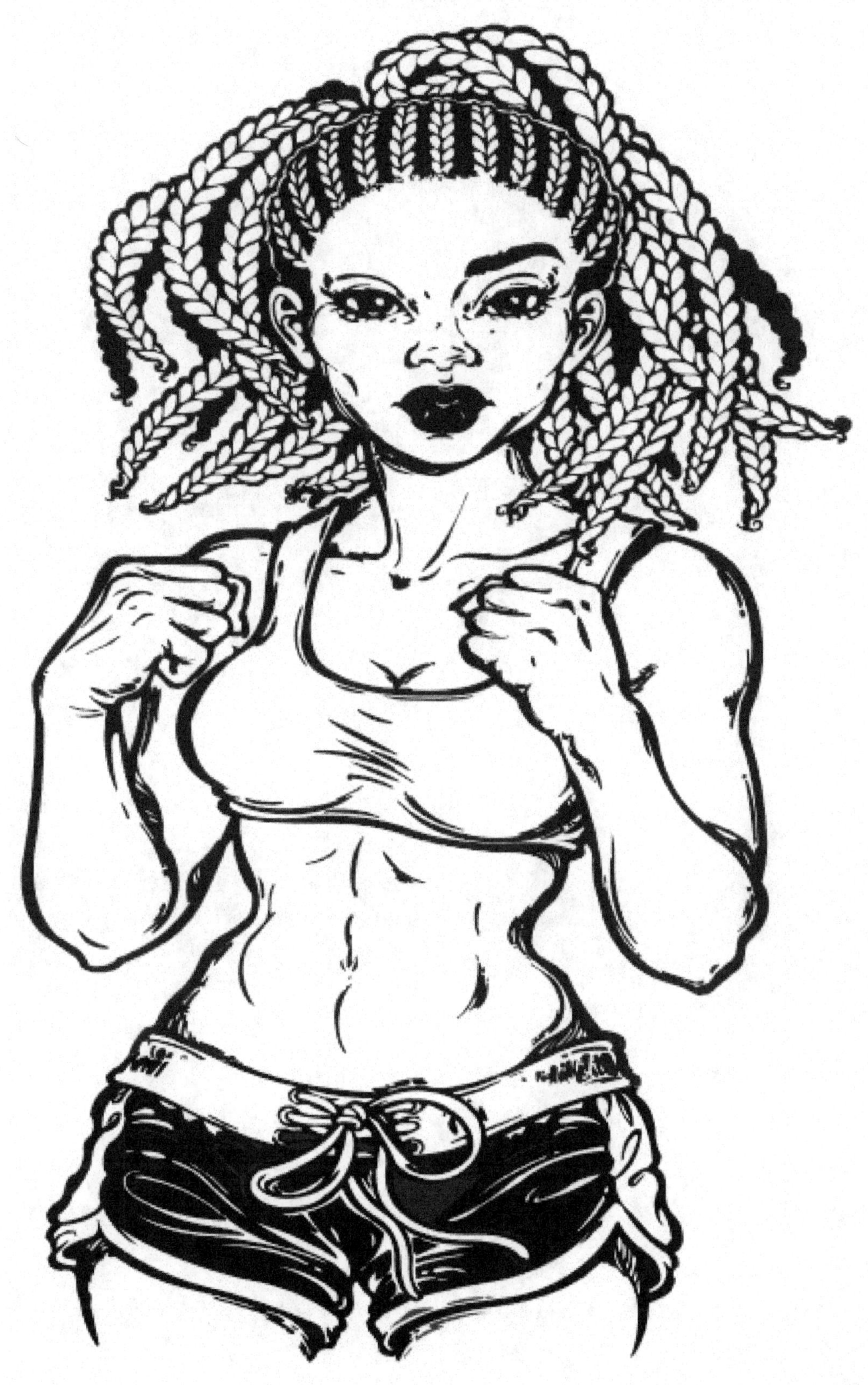

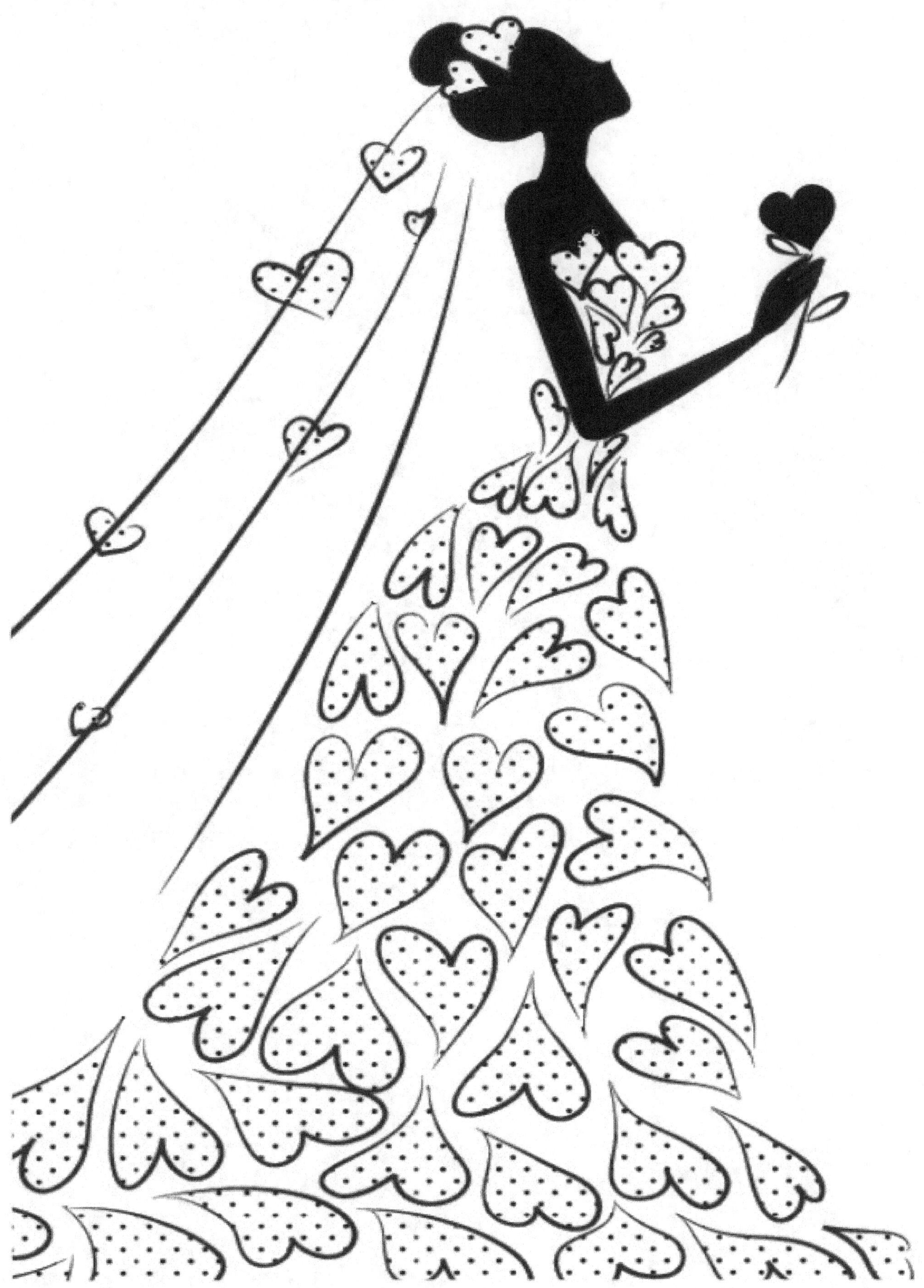

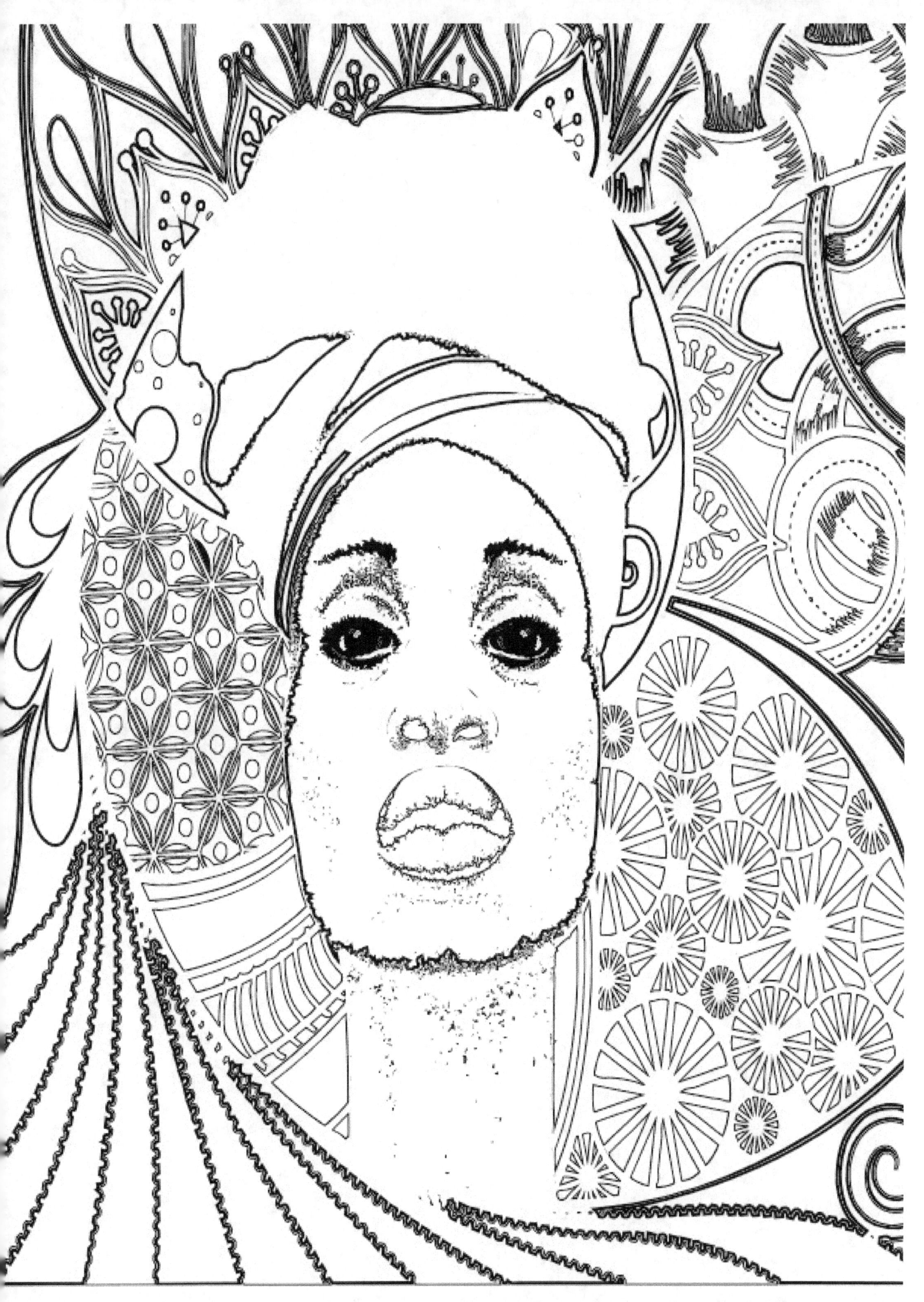

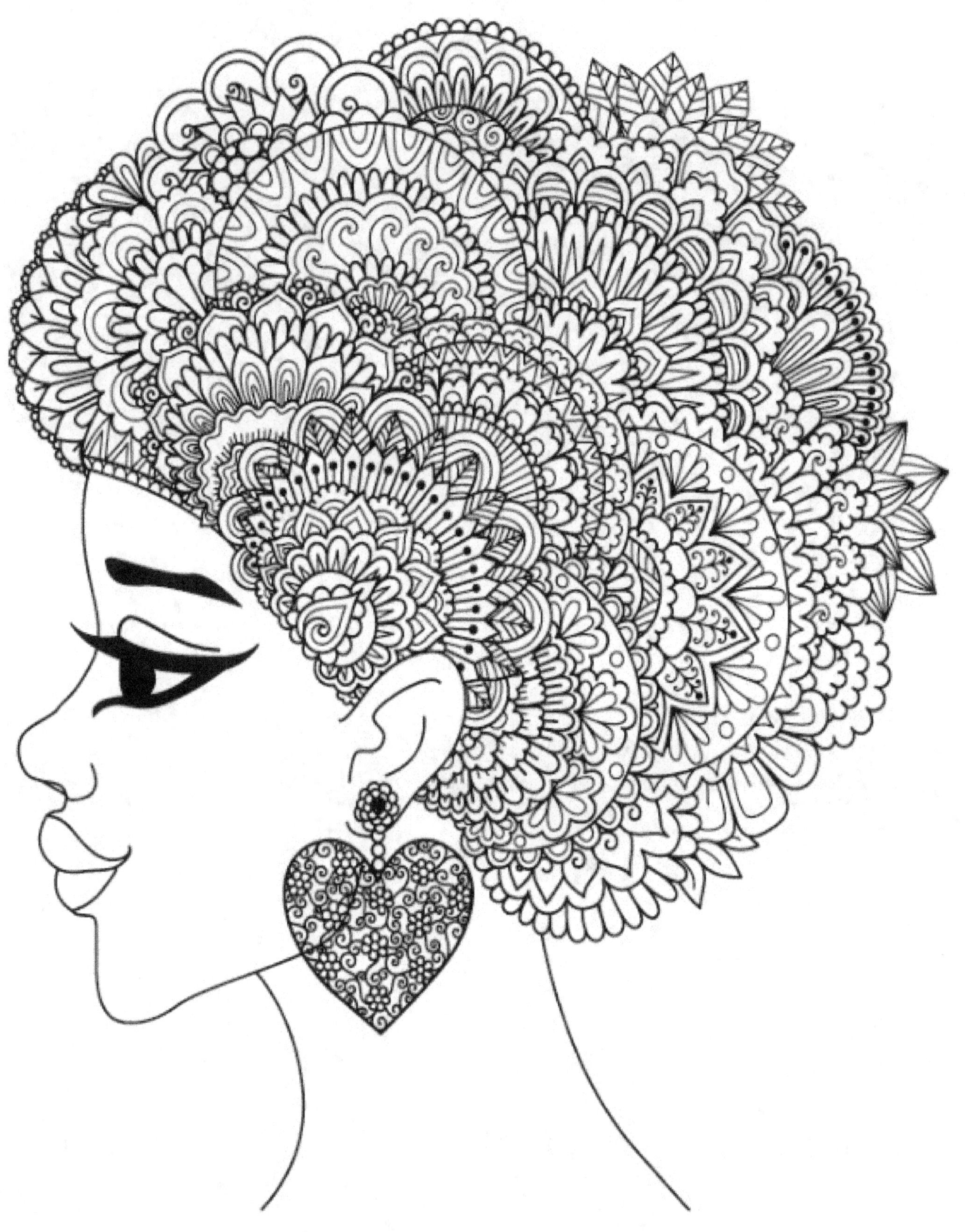

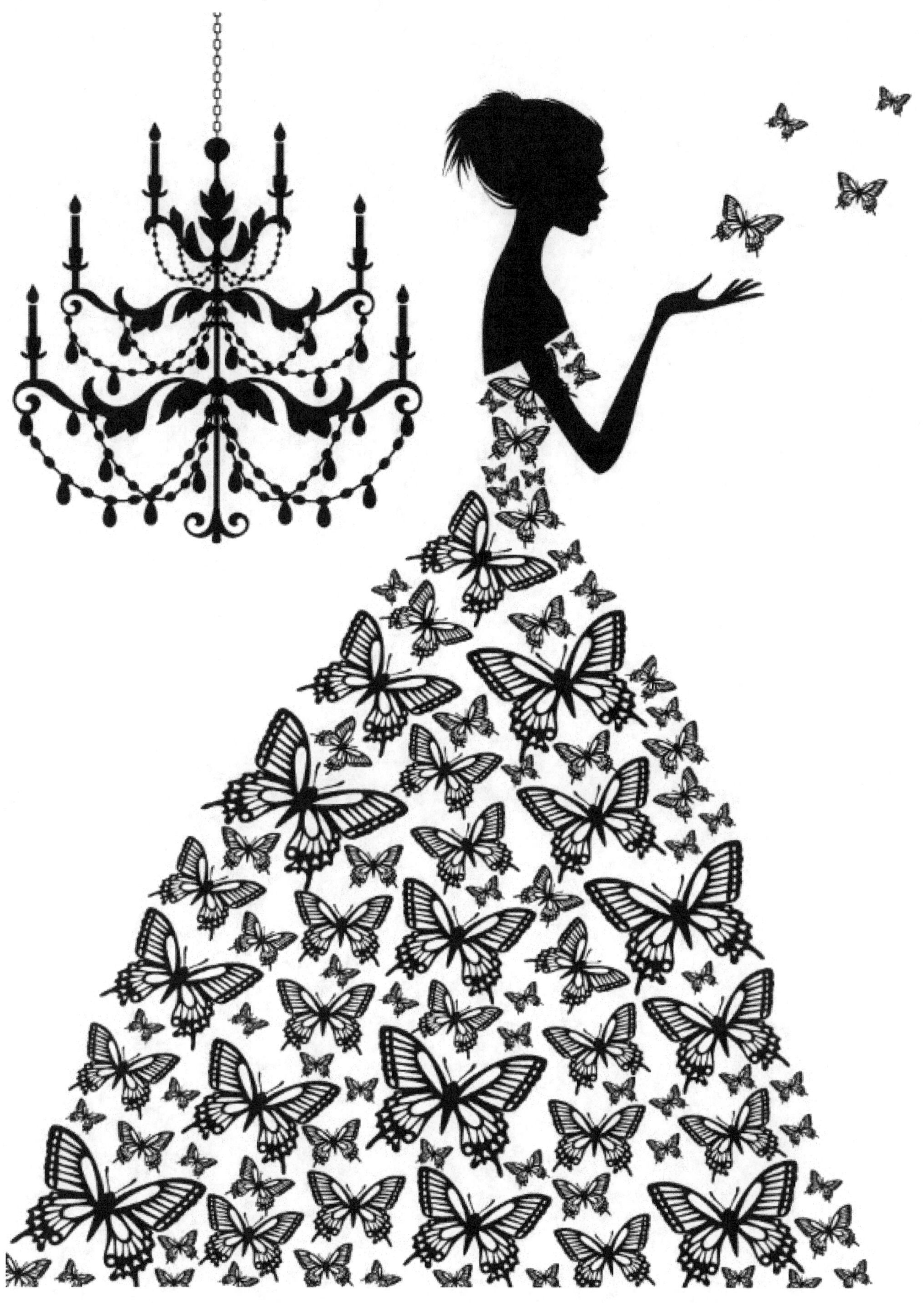

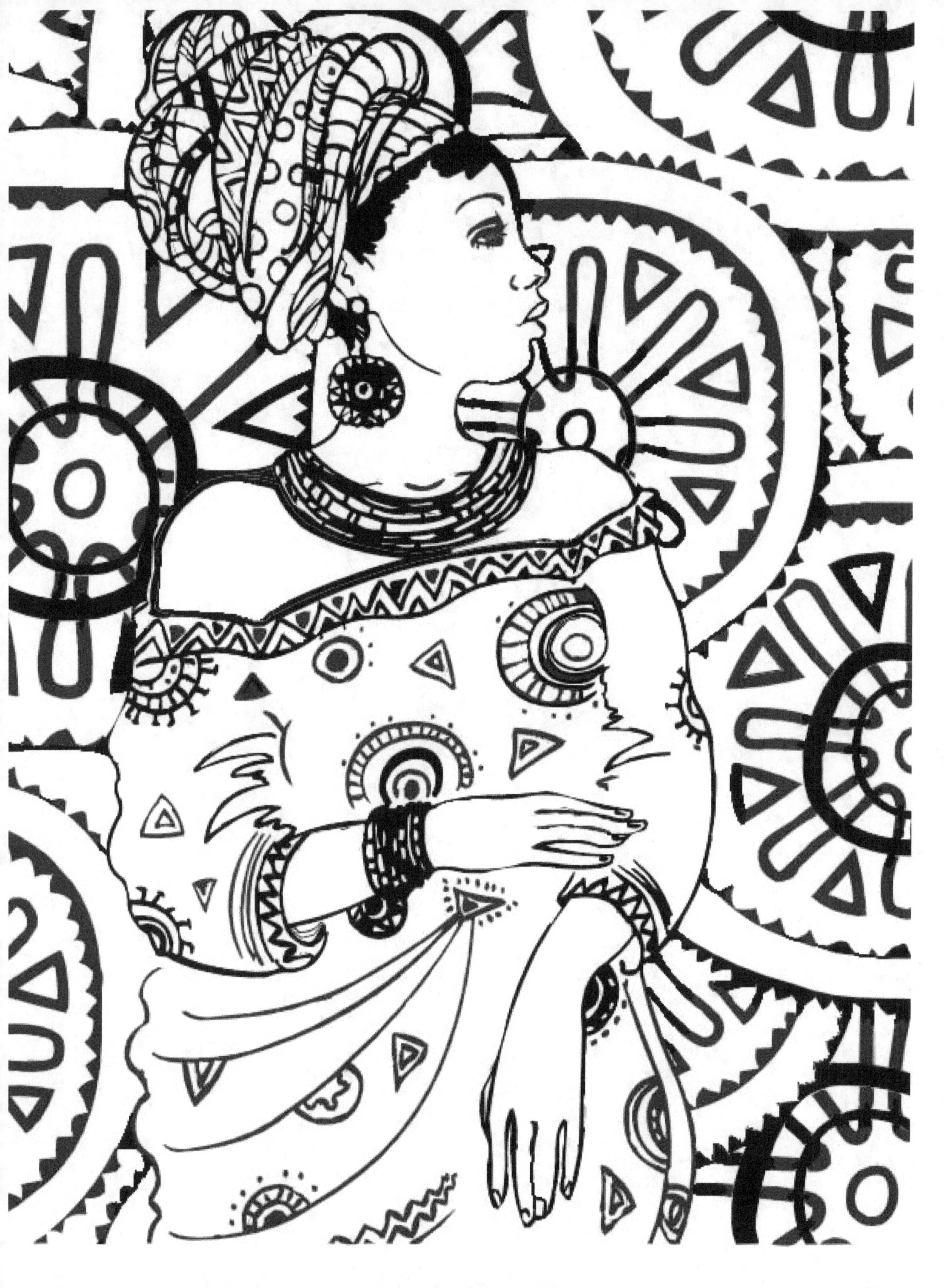

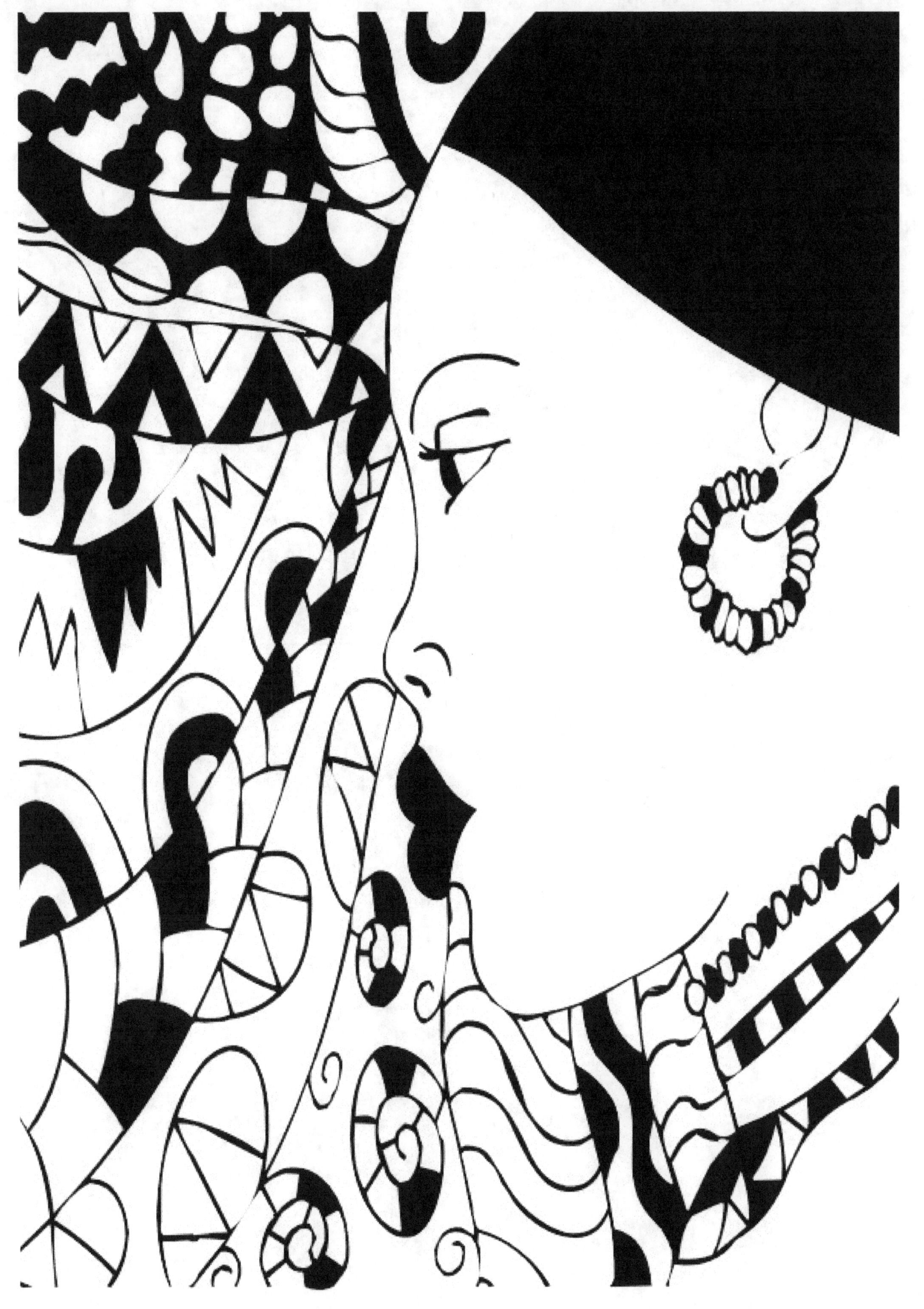

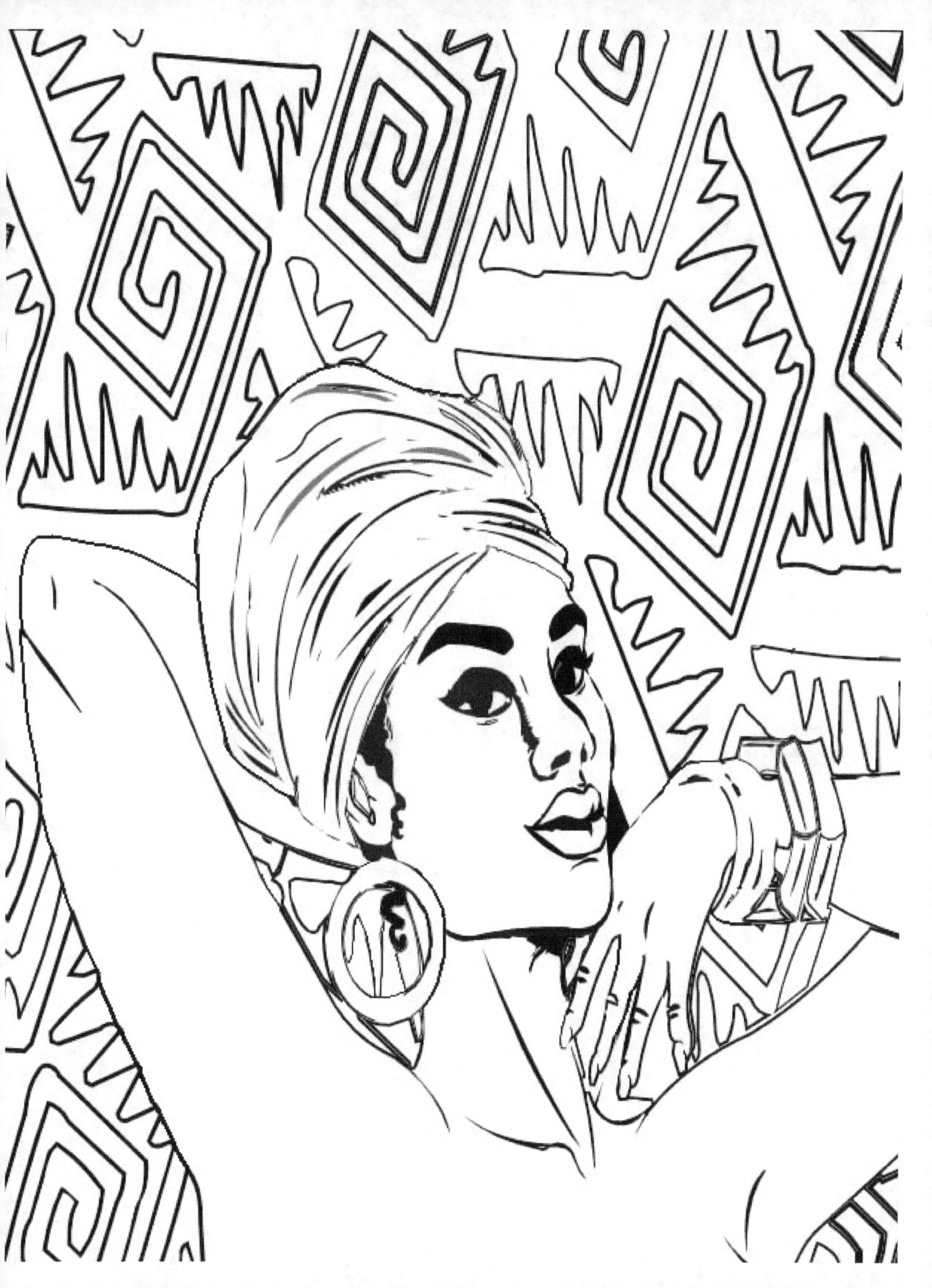

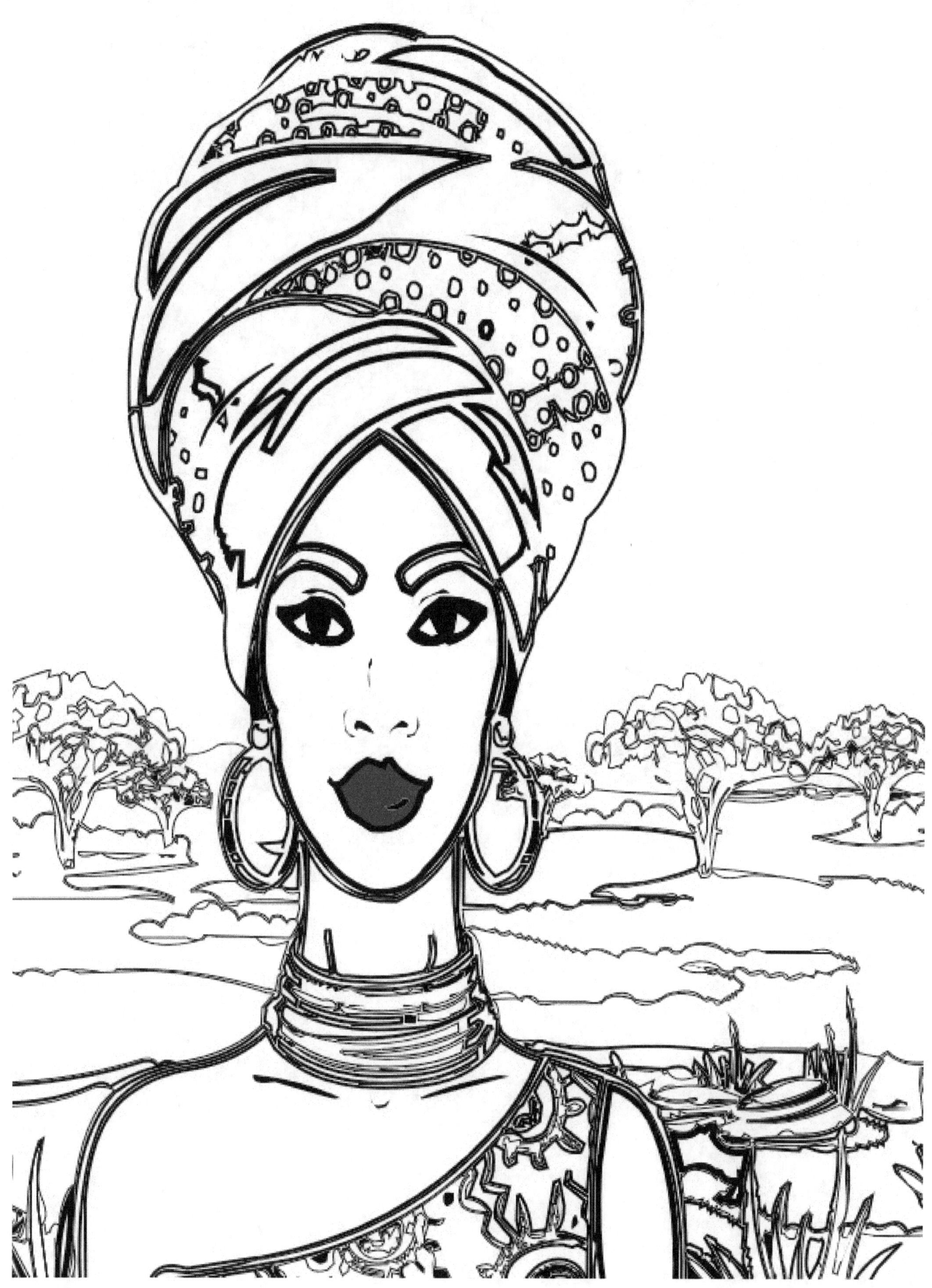

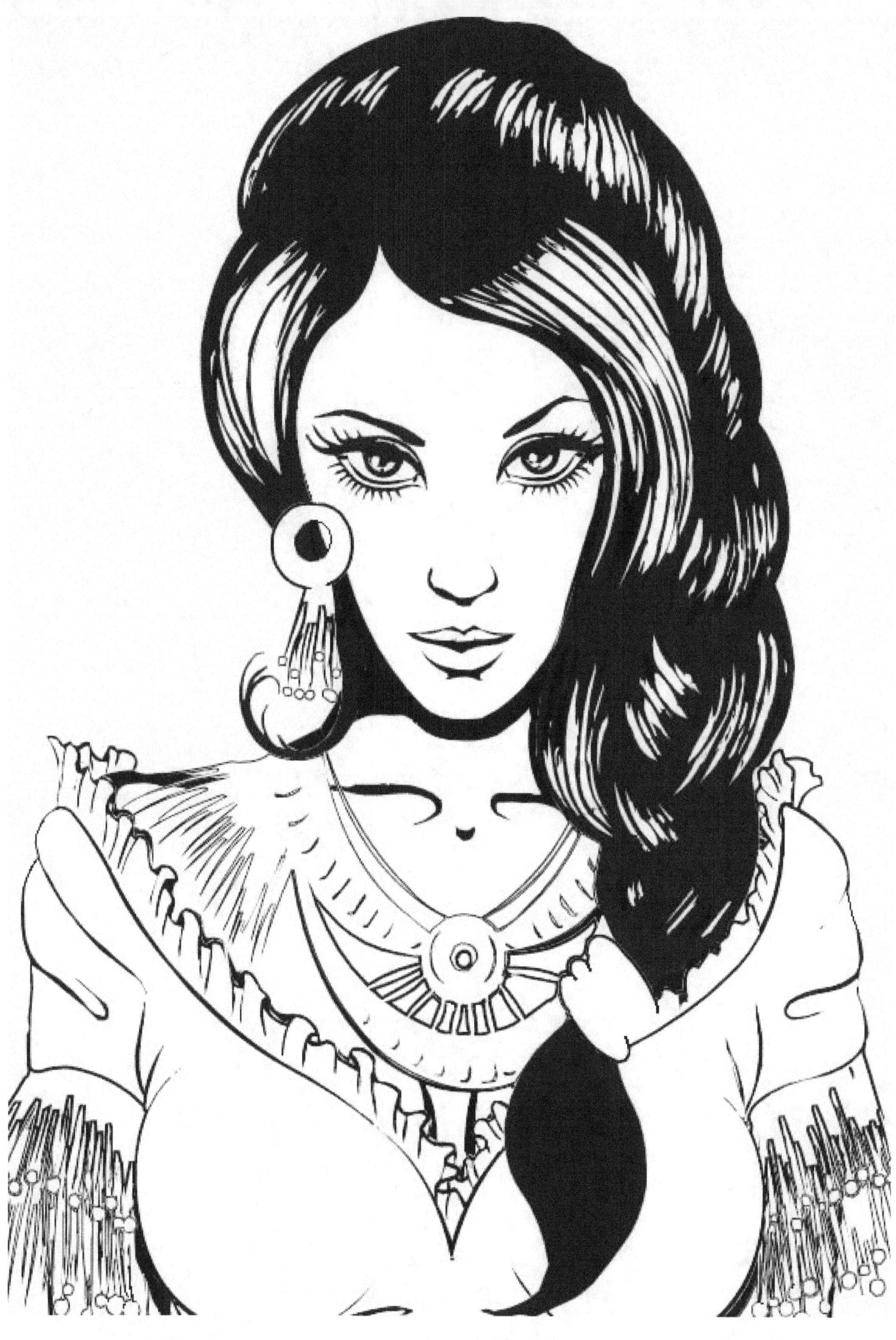

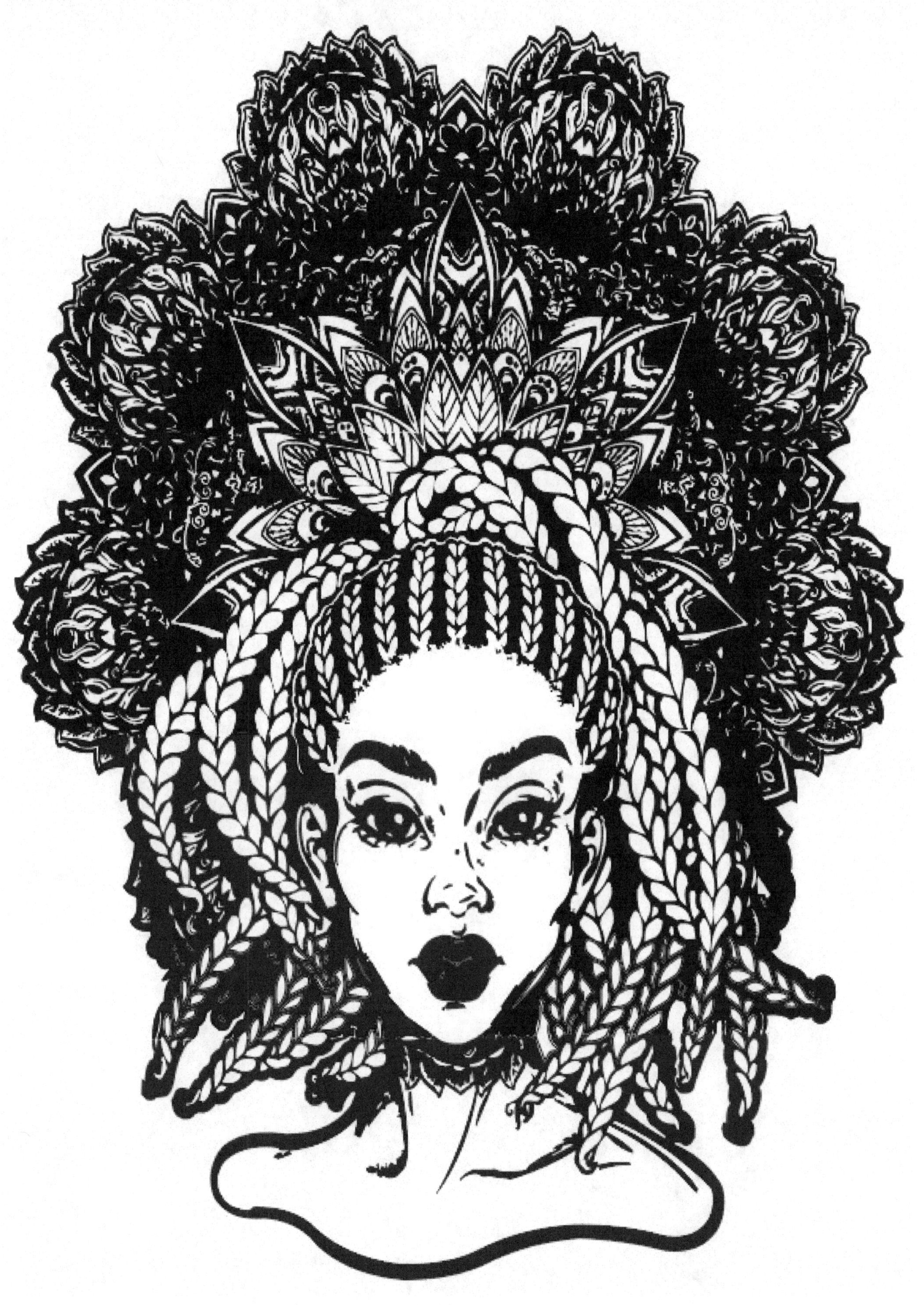

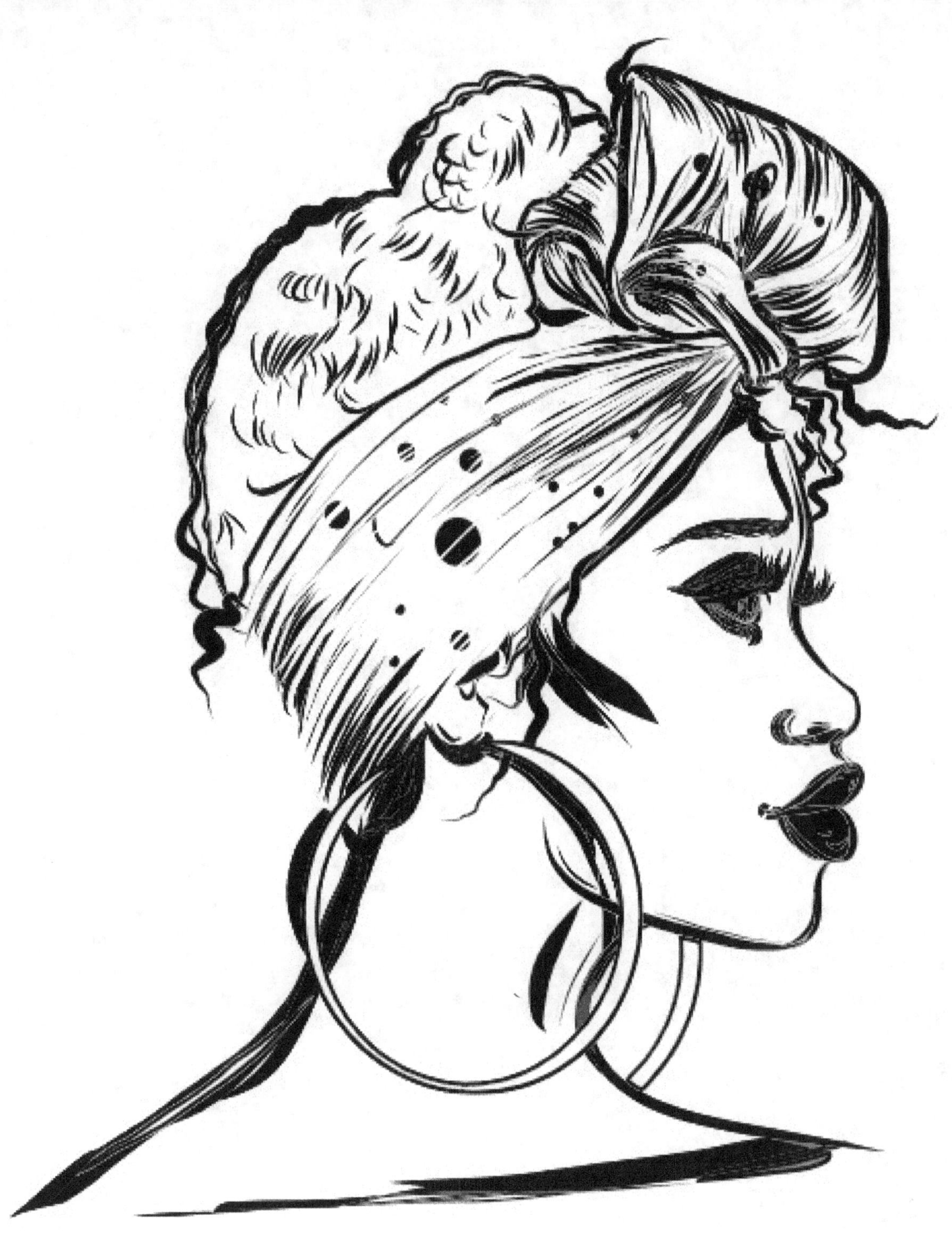

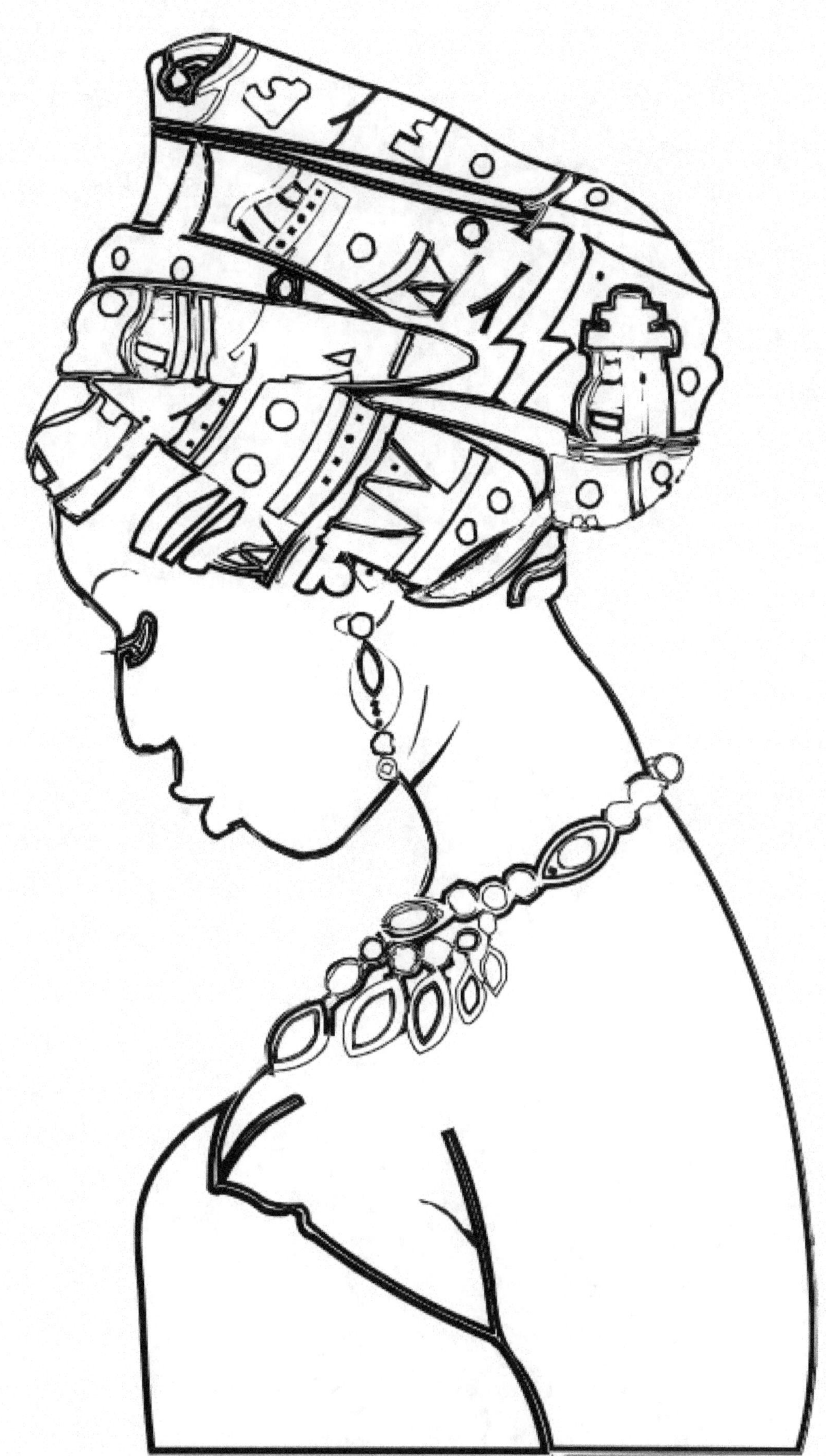

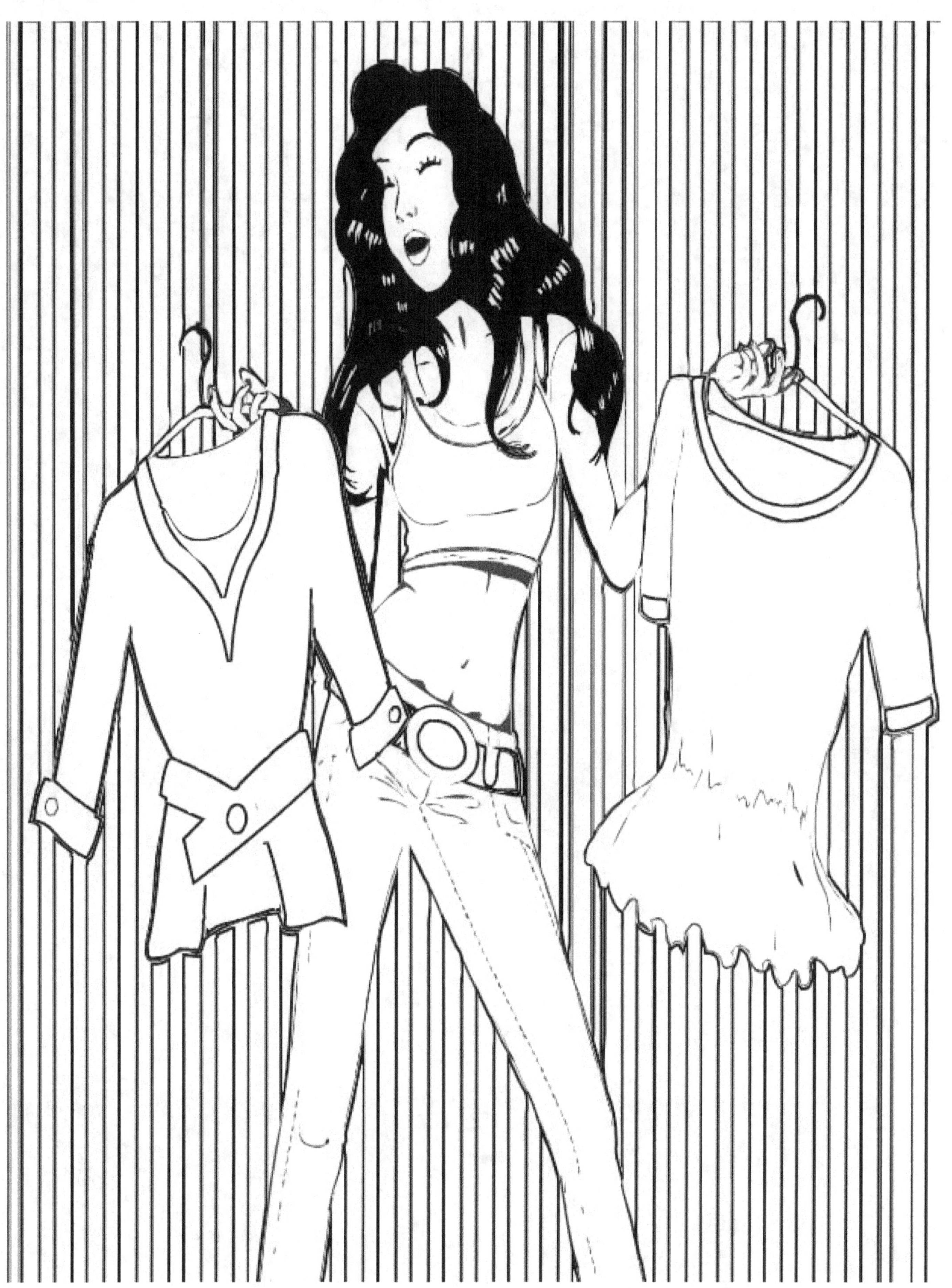

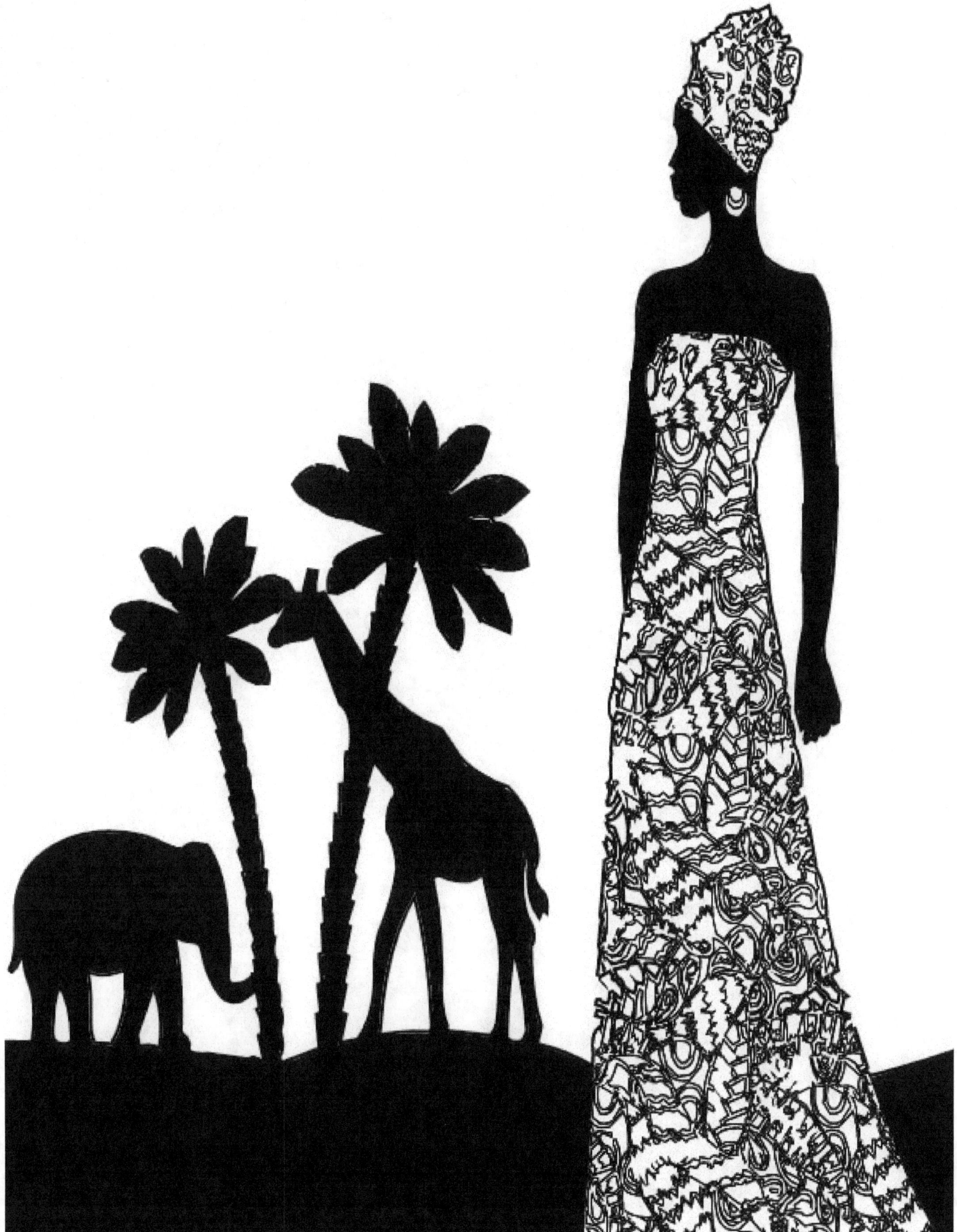

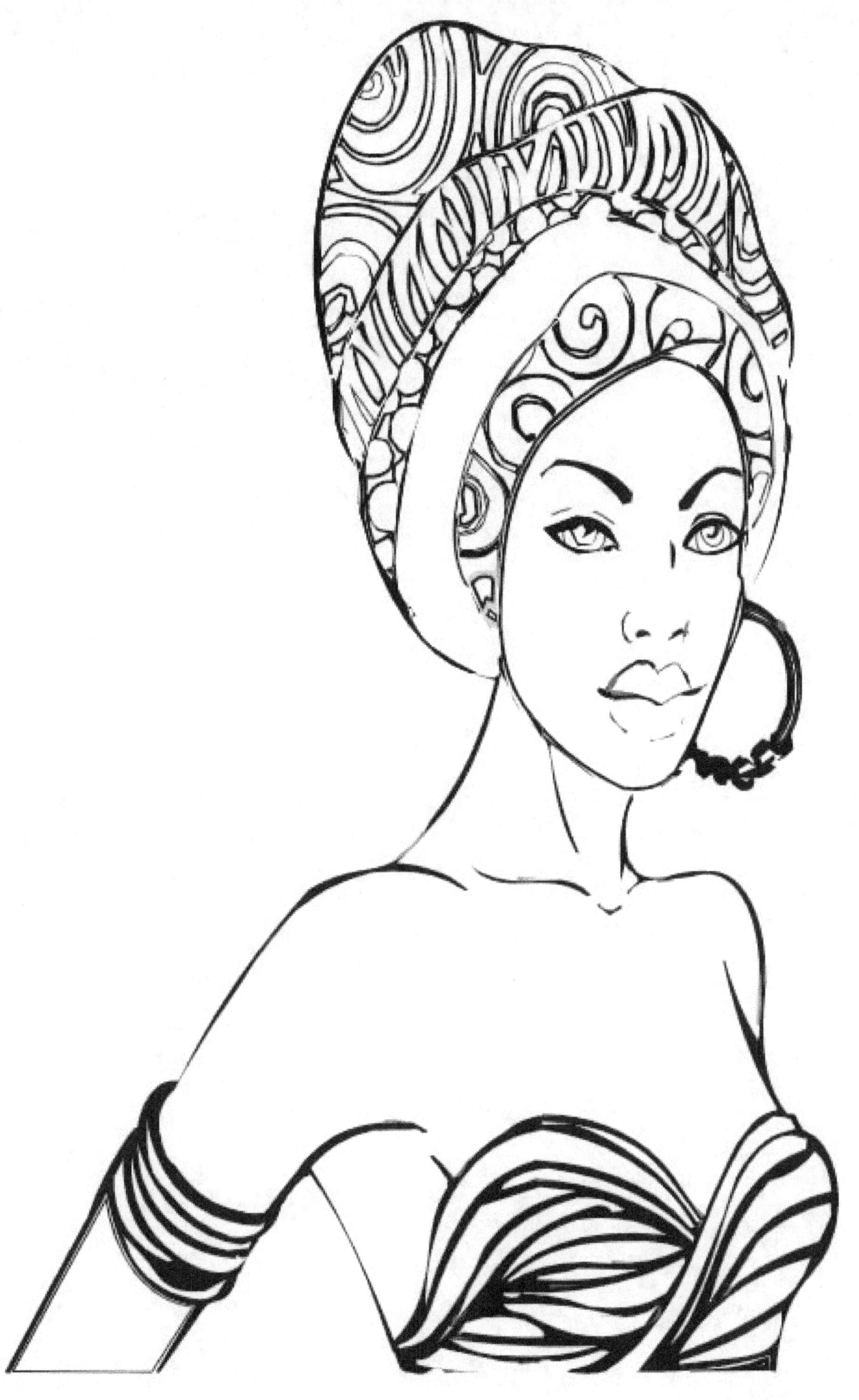

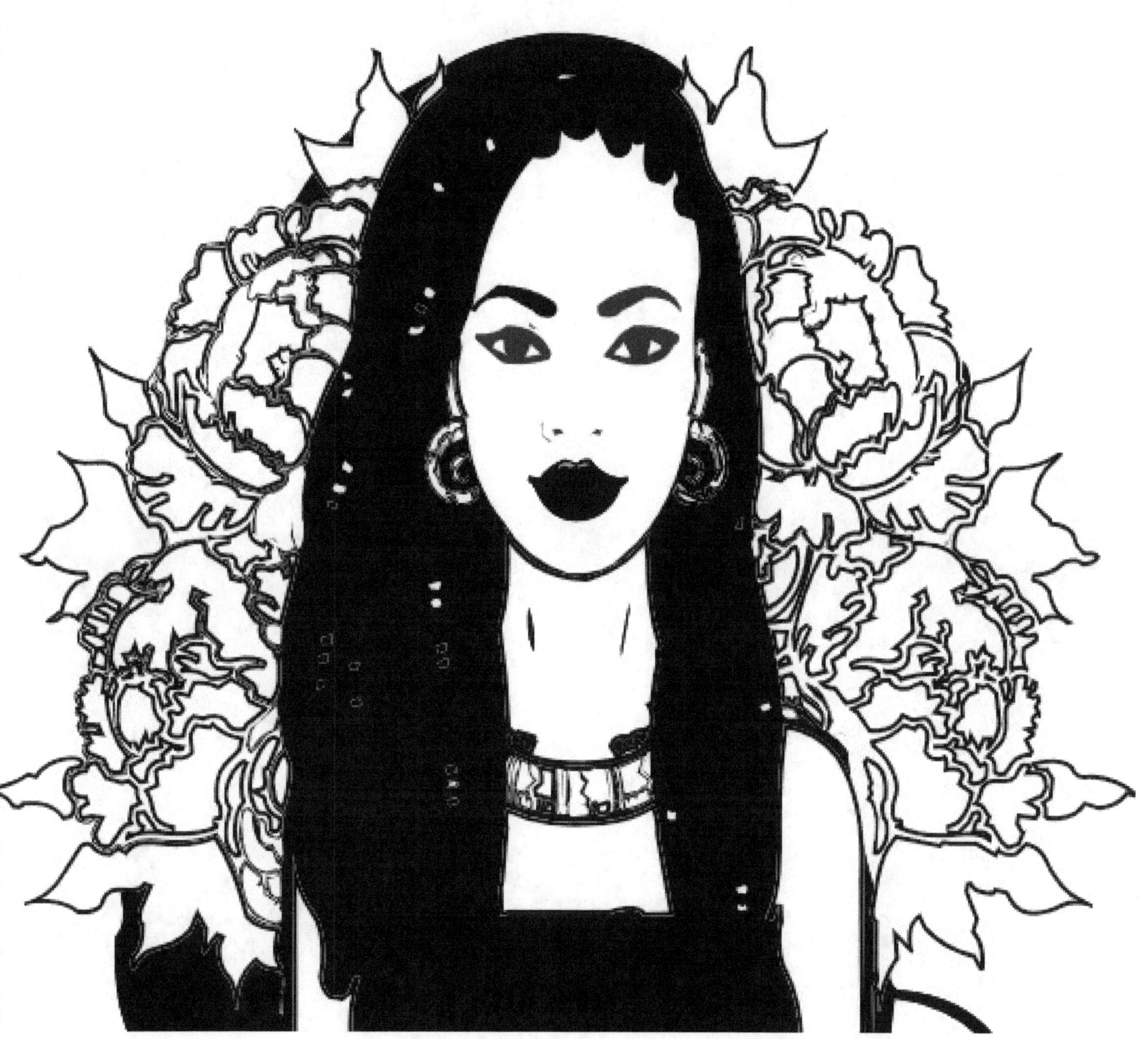

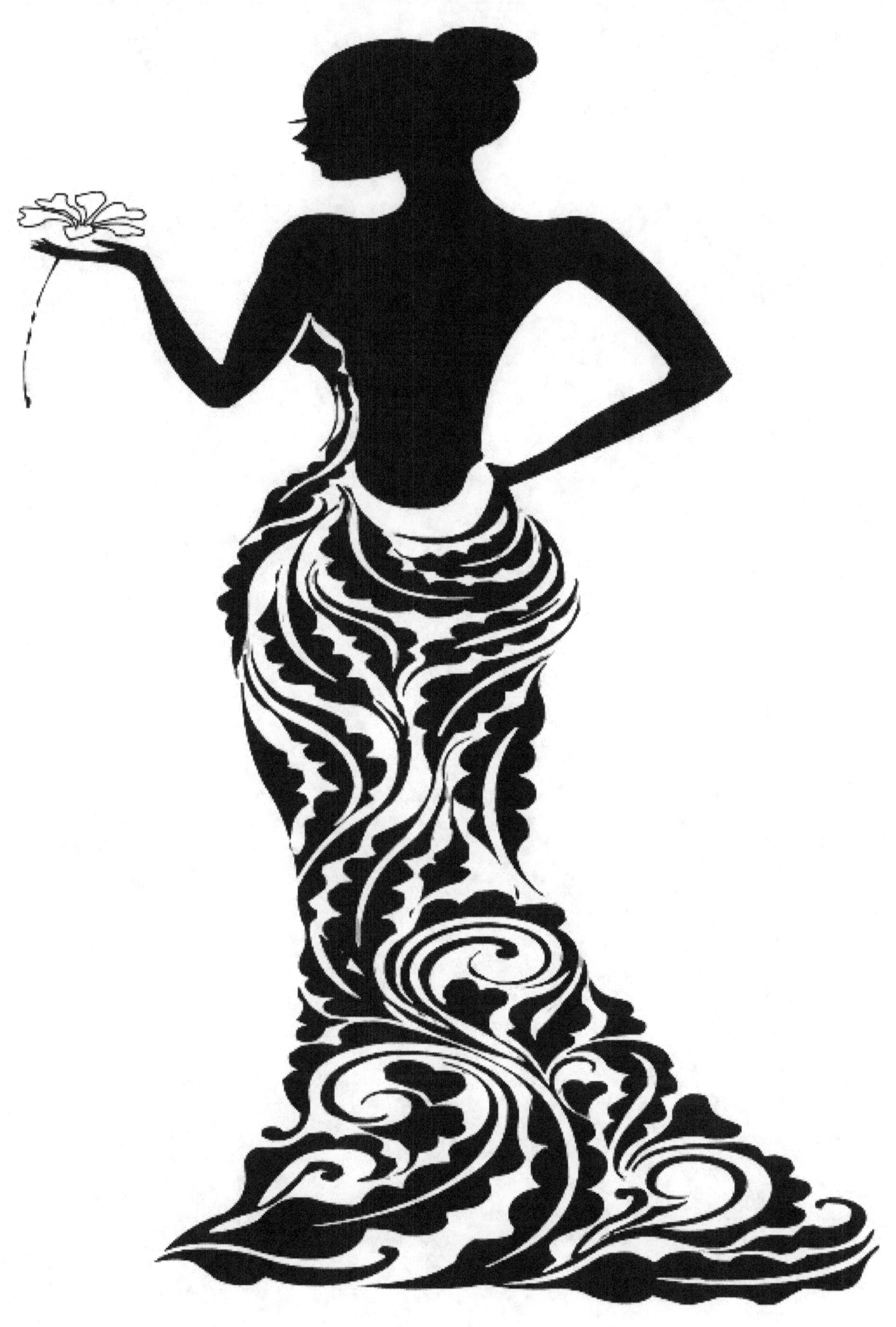

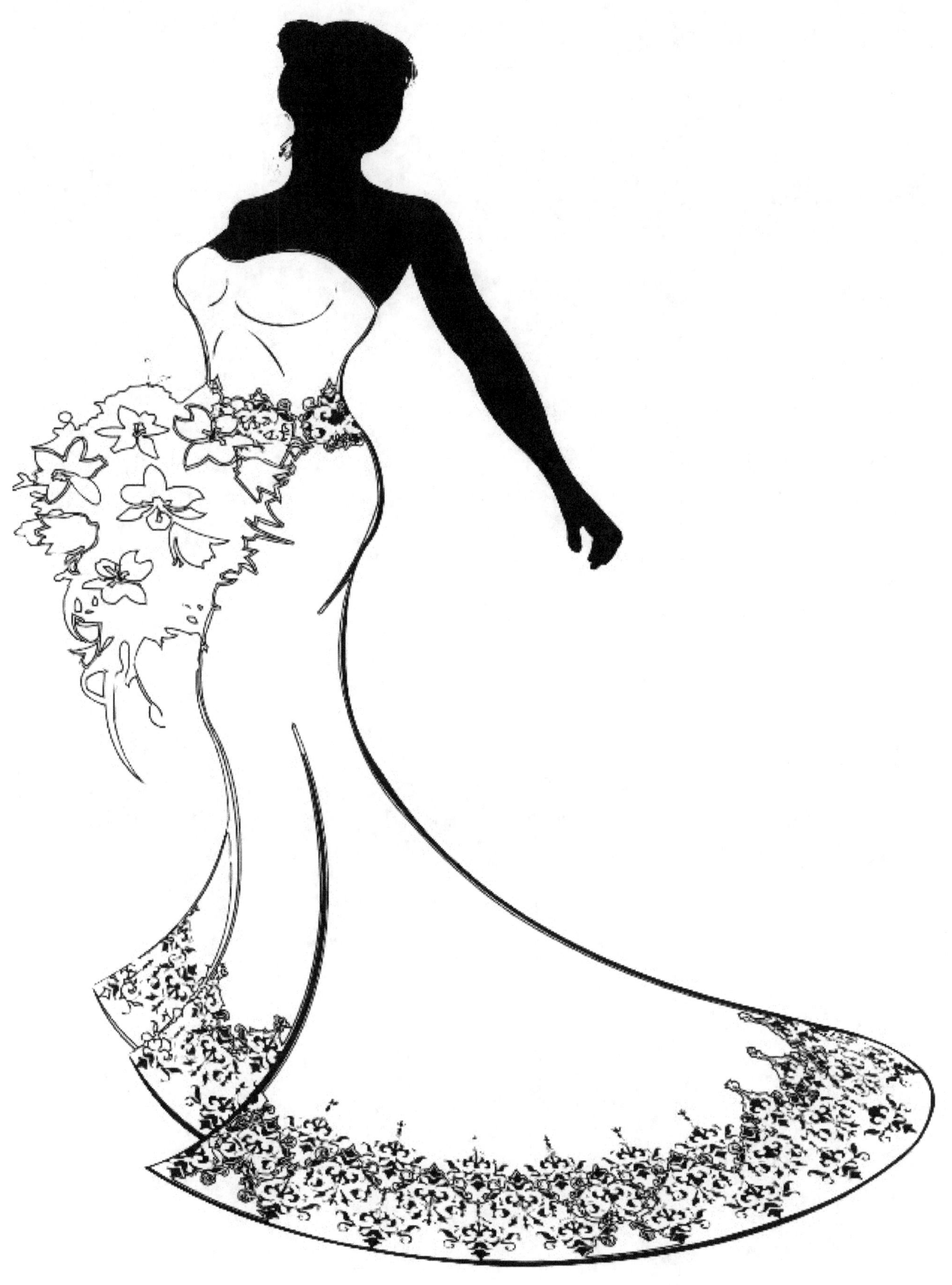